D1259666

Algrove Publishing Limited
36 Mill Street
Almonte, Ontario
Canada K0A 1A0

Telephone: (613) 256-0350
Fax: (613) 256-0360
Email: sales@algrove.com

National Library of Canada Cataloguing in Publication

    Skeleton leaves and phantom flowers.

(Classic reprint series)
Reprint. First published: Boston : J.E. Tilton, 1864.
Includes index.
ISBN 1-894572-91-2

    1. Floral decorations. 2. Leaves--Collection and preservation.
3. Flowers--Collection and preservation. I. Series: Classic reprint series
(Almonte, Ont.)

SB447.S54 2004   745.92   C2003-905705-4

Printed in Canada
#11003

Publisher's Note

It is necessary to remember, as you read this, that writers in the Victorian era often adopted a style of pomposity and prolixity (a pompous word!) that would not be tolerated today. Regardless of the writing style, the information in this small book is still very desirable.

We have taken the liberty of adding some modern recipes to the original text to update procedures. These are clearly separated from the original text, which has been faithfully reproduced, warts and all.

This reprint was undertaken at the suggestion of the Canadian Museum of Nature, which owns the 1864 original. Accordingly, it will receive royalties for copies sold.

Leonard G. Lee
Publisher
September 2003
Almonte, Ontario

PHANTOM FLOWERS,

A TREATISE

ON THE ART OF PRODUCING

SKELETON LEAVES

BOSTON:

J. E. TILTON AND COMPANY.

1864.

BOSTON:

STEREOTYPED BY THE BOSTON STEREOTYPE FOUNDRY.

Presswork by John Wilson and Son.

CONTENTS

		PAGE
	INTRODUCTION.	7
CHAP.		
I.	ANATOMY OF A LEAF. GREEN AND DRIED LEAVES.	15
II.	PREPARING THE LEAVES AND FLOWERS.	20
III.	BLEACHING THE LEAVES AND SEED-VESSELS.	29
IV.	ARRANGING THE BOUQUETS.	39
V.	ILLUSTRATED LIST OF PLANTS FOR SKELETONIZING.	48
VI.	SEED-VESSELS.	63
VII.	THE WONDERS AND USES OF A LEAF.	72
VIII.	LEAF PRINTING.	81
IX.	COMMERCIAL VALUE OF THE ART.	87
	PRESERVATION OF FLOWERS.	92
APPENDIX.		97

INTRODUCTION.

HANTOM BOUQUETS, so universally admired by all who can appreciate the chaste and beautiful in art, although but recently introduced to the notice of the American public, are no new thing.

The art of preparing the fibrous skeletons of plants was understood and practised by the Chinese many centuries ago, and there are still to be found in our fancy stores reasonably perfect specimens of these skeletonized leaves, generally painted and decorated with Oriental designs and mottoes, according to the taste of that remarkable people. Whether they have ever advanced so far as the grouping or arranging of these delicate tissues into anything approaching a bouquet, we cannot say; as no evidences of their faculty for producing such combinations have reached this country; or whether, if they had progressed so far, their stiff and awkward ideas of artistic effect would agree with the cultivated taste of Americans, remains to be imagined.

The works of Chinese art which reach us, whether on lacquered tables, work-boxes, waiters, &c., show how widely their conceptions of beautiful curves and graceful postures differ from our own standards of beauty. But be this as it may, American tourists, within the last few years, have been struck with the great beauty of these Phantom Bouquets, as exhibited in the fancy bazaars of European cities. These were evidently the work of the few who, in other lands than theirs, had acquired a knowledge of the art. A number of these bouquets

thus found their way to this country, where
they fortunately came under the notice of skilful
and cultivated minds, by whom the art of
producing them has been so patiently and
successfully pursued, that the specimens now
produced in this country surpass, in richness,
brilliancy, and faultless nicety of preparation
and arrangement, all that have been prepared
in foreign lands.

A recent English critic, in commenting on the
progress of the art, avers that leaf bleaching has
been known traditionally from time immemorial,
in Europe and Asia, by those families in which
botanical tastes have been hereditary. In Great
Britain and on the Continent, as well as in this
country, he says that among the quaint old curiosities to be found in the houses of retired sea-
captains, specimens of skeleton leaves are to be
found, covered with such pictures as only a
Chinese artist could execute. The process has
been described in London publications of the
seventeenth century, and was probably introduced into England from Italy during the reign

of Elizabeth. The critic concludes his historical summary with saying that "the fact so long known in Europe was circulated as a secret in Philadelphia in 1860!"

But greater secrets in the arts and sciences than the skeletonizing of a leaf, all exclusively of American origin, remain at this moment wholly unknown to the countrymen of the critic; while the particular art in question, when it had fairly attracted the notice of American taste and ingenuity, has in the brief period of five years received at American hands a more perfectly artistic development than all England was capable of accomplishing in two centuries. Accident alone has kept us in ignorance of an art distinguished only for its gracefulness; but the same accident keeps Europe profoundly ignorant of a multitude of processes, of every-day use with us, which lighten and economize human labor, and contribute largely, not only to public and private comfort, but to national wealth.

Five years ago the first Phantom Bouquet

ever offered for sale on this side of the Atlantic, was made by an American lady, and was exhibited in the spacious window of a large jewelry establishment in one of our chief cities. Although surrounded by flashing silver ware and sparkling gems, yet the little bouquet, composed of only a few leaves and flowers, attracted the highest admiration of all who beheld it, and as may be supposed, it soon found an appreciative purchaser at a high price. A few others (all that could then be furnished) were disposed of at the same establishment during that season. This public display served to awaken a wide interest in the subject, stimulating inquiry into the wonderful art by which the perishable leaves and blossoms of the forest and the garden are converted into durable illustrations of the complex structure of the floral world.

As is usual with so decided a novelty, many amateurs were ready to experiment the following year. Among numerous lamentable failures, a few only were partially successful in their attempts to reproduce them. We say partially, for in many cases a fine leaf was marred by stains or spots, or blemishes occasioned by the ravages of insects; and although otherwise it may have been perfectly skeletonized, and the shape preserved entire and beautiful, yet these blemishes served to spoil the effect, and to destroy its value for a bouquet. Many of the less particular artists did not hesitate to mix a few of such defective specimens in their arrangements; but most persons of correct taste preferred to group gracefully their half dozen perfect leaves under a small shade, than to make a towering bouquet of imperfect or dis-colored ones.

The time which has elapsed since the art was first introduced here has been a season of patient experiment and investigation. There were no published essays to which the learner could refer for directions. All must be studied and acquired by laborious and careful observa-tion, and often whole seasons would be lost while ascertaining the peculiar properties of a single leaf, the process being too slow to allow of a second gathering before Autumn had stripped the trees.

The first summer of the writer's experiments was lost in vain attempts; and bushels of carefully gathered leaves were wasted for want of a few items of knowledge, which, to a careless operator, would seem of small importance. Five years of practice have taught her many things indispensable to a successful prosecution of the art, such as are neither understood nor appreciated by those who have just commenced the work. It is the object of these pages to furnish plain and practical directions for producing perfect Bouquets of Skeleton Flowers, together with a list of such plants as will repay the artist's labor.

A late writer on this subject enthusiastically declares that the art is yet in its infancy, and expresses his belief that diligent experiment will lead to results even more wonderful than any that have yet been achieved. In the confident belief that such will be the case, we shall feel glad to have given our readers an impulse in the right direction, and can assure them that by closely following the rules here given, success will certainly reward their efforts. Those whom repeated failures may have so far discouraged as to induce them to abandon the pursuit, will be stimulated to renew their interesting labors. Others, whose entire ignorance of the process may have withheld them from even beginning, will be induced to make a trial. The probability is, that among the aspirants thus stimulated to enter the field, some superior genius will be found, at whose animating touch this beautiful art will receive a brilliancy of development surpassing all that could have been imagined by those who pioneered it into public notice.

ANATOMY OF A LEAF; GREEN AND DRIED LEAVES.

ANCIFUL, though expressive, is the appellation of "Phantom" or "Spiritual" Flowers; it was given to the first American specimens by those who produced them, and it has since become so general as to be everywhere understood and accepted as their most appropriate name.

Referring to the process by which these flowers are prepared, a Christian friend of the author very beautifully used them as emblems of the Resurrection, and as illustrating the ideas, — " Sown a natural body, raised a spiritual body," and, " this corruptible must put on incorruption, and this mortal immortality."

The process through which the green and healthy leaves must pass is literally one of corruption, for during the warm summer days, as the work goes slowly on, they become blackened and offensive, and often infested with insects; and yet these conditions are absolutely necessary to secure their final and perfect beauty. But when the work of corruption and decay is fully accomplished, there remains after all, in the midst of that disgusting compound of offensive odors and green slime, the beautifully faultless framework of leaves and flowers, ready to be rescued and purified. On the conduct of this portion of the work, and the subsequent cleansing and bleaching of the delicate tissues, the whole thing depends. The operator may consider herself eminently successful if she is able to present, as finished specimens, one half the number of leaves originally gathered. Yet if a single bouquet of perfect phantoms, white and clear of blemishes, should result from the summer's labor, she will feel herself abundantly compensated for her pains, and may delight her eyes for many years to come with this unfading remembrancer of the localities from which they may have been gathered, or of the friends who may have assisted in the pleasing employment.

The substance of these curious leaf-tissues is gen-

erally classed by botanists under two distinct heads —
the vascular, or veinwork, and the cellular, or intermediate green matter which fills up the interstices and
gives coherence and solidity to the leaf. In undertaking to produce these skeleton leaves, the great
problem is how best to destroy and remove the cellular and more perishable portion, while we preserve
intact the network of veins or nerves by which the
whole is kept in shape, and which perform the same
office in the leaf-structure as the nerves and veins
within the human body.

Different parties will generally be found to have different ways of doing the same thing. While we shall
endeavor faithfully to describe that which is probably
the more popular plan, we shall, nevertheless, give the
preference to the slow but sure process which our own
experience has proved to be the most reliable.

The traveller who visits localities which have been
celebrated in history, or made immortal by the visita-
tions of the muse, desires to preserve some mementoes
of his pilgrimage to scenes so hallowed. The most
simple as well as the most usual keepsakes, are sprays
of leaves or flowers, pressed between the pages of a
book, for future preservation in the album or the port-
folio. But all green leaves, when thus pressed and

dried, become very brittle, and will break upon the slightest attempt to fold or bend them. If placed in vases, they will soon curl and lose their color, compelling their early dismissal from the parlor. Not so after passing through the skeletonizing process. They then become strong and flexible, may be folded or bent in any way desired, and, although appearing to be so frail and delicate, will, in most cases, bear a considerable amount of handling and pressure without tearing. Yet it will be seen by the directions which follow these preliminary remarks, that the greatest care is required to manipulate the fragile fabrics, as the slightest pull in the wrong way, or the neglect of precautions and rules, which to the learner may seem unimportant, may spoil the most promising attempts, and disappoint the hopes and expectations of an entire season.

This is especially true in regard to the bleaching process. During the first season of the writer's experiments, whole jars of perfect specimens were lost in passing through this stage of the preparation, in consequence of her ignorance of the true method, subsequently acquired by patient and careful study. Having now ascertained the proper method of proceeding, it is a rare thing to lose a leaf, or even a spray of fern, the latter being, perhaps, the most difficult of preparation, because of its exquisite delicacy of structure, in both respects exceeding any in the list of plants that we shall give hereafter, while it is indispensable to the complete and graceful bouquet.

PREPARING THE LEAVES AND FLOWERS.

HEN Spring has once more dressed both tree and shrub in their gorgeous livery of green, the artist begins to look around her for the most suitable subjects for experiment. The influence of the new study on her mind becomes immediately apparent to herself. The trees, which have heretofore appeared to her as presenting an unbroken uniformity of foliage, now display their leaves to her sharpened observation with a wealth of capabilities before unknown to her, and she is surprised to learn how infinite a variety exists in the vegetable world; variety, not only in size and outline, but in those other characteristics which are so

(20)

important to her purpose, strength of fibre, and free-
dom from blemishes occasioned by the destructive ravages of insects.   As observation is directed to the
subject, so the mind becomes expanded under the influence of the new study.   The surprising difference
between the leaves now first becomes apparent. They
are seen to be serrated or entire, ovate, accuminate,
cordate, or irregular. The magnificent luster of the
Ivy and the Magnolia now, for the first time, attract
attention, and secure for them a new admiration. As
the season advances, she will be struck with the numerous changes to which the leaves are subject, before
the chill winds of Autumn strip them from the trees,
thence depositing them in rustling piles upon the
ground. As incidental to the study, the habits of a
multitude of insect depredators will be noticed, affording new subjects for surprise, and fresh accessions of
knowledge.   Everywhere the wonders of the Divine
Hand will be displayed under conditions to which she
had been a stranger; and the mysteries of Nature, thus
unfolded, will infinitely surpass all which these pages
can be made to contain.

Without some directions to guide her, the enthusias-
tic learner, in haste to begin the work, gathers indis-
criminately from forest and garden, selecting leaves

remarkable only for their ample size or pleasing shape, and places the whole diversified collection in the prepared receptacle to undergo the process of maceration. In her ignorance of certain first principles, she does not imagine that she has overlooked some of the most indispensable ingredients of success, which, standing as they do at the very threshold of the undertaking, must not only influence, but, when disregarded, must render absolutely futile all subsequent steps in a process which, under any circumstances, is exceedingly tedious. We may suppose that in her natural impatience to commence her labors she has gathered up an ample store of leaves, immediately on their attaining their full growth. It is true that in this early preparation she has anticipated the attacks of destructive insects, but the leaf will then be too immature to withstand the macerating process. The fibres will be found too succulent, and not sufficiently ligneous, to sustain the pressure and handling always necessary to produce a perfectly skeletonized leaf. After probably two months of patient watchfulness, she is consequently compelled to throw away her choice collection, the whole having become a mass of pulp, in which there is neither stem nor fibre to identify a single leaf.

By this time the season has advanced, and the

foliage on the trees has undergone important changes. Many of the leaves having lost their early succulency, have assumed a strong ligneous character. In place of excessive pulpiness, an undue proportion of fibre pervades the whole structure of the leaf. It has, in fact, become too old for maceration. In other cases the leaf has been either stung by an insect, and the channels through which the sap so mysteriously circulates having become obstructed by the poisonous infusion injected into them, its shape becomes distorted, or its surface is disfigured by blisters. Others have been attacked by a different tribe of enemies, who, by half devouring the leaf, as effectually destroy it for the artist. The latter catastrophe invariably overtakes the foliage of the Elm, the Magnolia, and the Maple. These facts we have verified in our own experience; and having been compelled thus to learn them, the resulting knowledge was acquired only from repeated and trying disappointments. They make evident the importance of knowing the exact point in the season at which each leaf is in proper condition for the artist's hand.

Another error consists in placing in the macerating vessel many different sorts of leaves, without a knowledge of their chemical properties. For instance, those of the Oak, Chestnut, Walnut, Birch, and Hickory contain so large a quantity of tannin as to render it almost impossible to macerate them in the usual way. If placed among other and more perishable leaves, the infusion of tannin thus created will act as a preservative, and entirely prevent their decomposition. The writer learned these facts, to her cost, during the first season's experiments. A few beautiful Oak leaves were placed among a large number of other varieties which were in course of preparation, and not until after months of patient waiting, watchfulness, and handling did she discover the true cause of her disappointment, when it was too late in the season to repair the loss. The reader will at once perceive how important are these rules and cautions, thus placed at the head of our directions.

Throughout the Middle States, by the fifteenth of June, most of the desirable leaves will be found fully grown, and many of them are then old enough to gather. Elms, Swamp Magnolias, Maples, Deutzias, Pears, Silver Poplars, and English Sycamores may be selected, but none but the firmest and most perfect leaves should be taken. These kinds may be placed together in open vessels and covered with soft water, and then set in a warm or sunny place in the open air. A broad weight may be placed on the top, so as to insure continued immersion. A newspaper, doubled and laid over the top of the leaves, will answer the same purpose as a weight, and is perhaps better, as it keeps its place, while the weight sometimes falls to the bottom of the vessel. The best vessel for the purpose is a common earthen jar with a wide mouth, the size to be proportioned to the quantity of leaves to be macerated.

At the end of six weeks the paper may be removed, and a few of the leaves carefully taken out for examination, and placed in a basin of clean warm water. To do this, the human hand is the best instrument; but, as many persons may object to thus dipping into what has now become an unpleasant mass of vegetable decomposition, a broad wooden spoon may be substituted. Then, taking a leaf between the thumb and finger, immerse the hand in the warm water, and press and rub the leaf either gently or firmly, according to the strength of its texture. This rubbing process will remove the loose green matter from the surface, and expose to view the fibrous network of the leaf. With those which are strongest, especially the Swamp Magnolias, a brush will be needed to effectually clean them, — a soft tooth-brush will answer best, — but in using a brush, the leaf should be laid in the palm of the hand, on a plate, or on any other surface equally flat and smooth.

This constitutes the first washing, and a few of the leaves will now be found perfectly clear. But to some of them thus washed and but partially cleared, further care must be extended. It will, therefore, be necessary to have at hand a second vessel of water similar to the first, in which all such imperfectly skeletonized leaves may be placed, where they must remain until finished, which, with all but the Swamp Magnolias, will probably be two or three weeks longer.

We may suppose that the artist has made a beginning with the leaves already mentioned in this chapter. On taking them out of the macerating vessel, and washing them as directed, she will find the Deutzias and Silver Poplars perfectly clean, and they should then be placed in a basin of clean water, until all the contents of the macerating jar have been examined. A few of the Norway Maples will also be found perfectly prepared; but the majority of all contained in the jar will still be only partially so.

In the latter condition will be found the Sycamores, the Silver Maples, the Elms, and the Pears. These must, consequently, be deposited in the second vessel, as before mentioned, to undergo still further maceration. The Magnolias will require another two or three months' soaking before the outer cuticle will become soft enough to remove; but, if more convenient, they may be placed in the same vessel with those last named. After covering these half-cleaned leaves with water, all in different stages of progress, they should be left in the same warm, sunny place to be finished. We may here remark, for the comfort of the learner who has persevered thus far in an operation which will be discovered to be decidedly unpleasant to her olfactory organs, that the most offensive portion of the labor is over, at least with this particular set of leaves, as after having received their first washing, they part with most of the putrefactive odors which have so long pervaded the air in the vicinity of the macerating jar.

The clear and perfect leaves which were deposited in the clean water, awaiting a leisure hour to give them further attention, may now be deprived of their moisture by carefully pressing them between the folds of a soft towel until they are perfectly dry. On no account let them be laid on a table, or other hard surface, while in a wet state, as in drying they will adhere to it so closely as to tear in the effort to remove them. The Norway Maple, being extremely delicate, will adhere, while wet, even to the hand, and great care must be exercised in removing its leaves to avoid tearing. It will be noticed that many of the leaves will lose their stems in passing through the process; but the mode by which this deficiency is to be supplied, will be explained in its proper place hereafter. When dried, the leaves may be placed in boxes, ready for bleaching when the assortment has been completed.

CHAPTER III.

BLEACHING THE LEAVES AND SEED VESSELS.

THE next process, and one of great importance, is that of bleaching the leaves, flowers, and seed-vessels. It is an operation which requires the greatest care, as upon the perfect whiteness of all the component parts of a bouquet its beauty will depend. No matter how perfectly the leaves and seed-vessels may have been skeletonized, if they are permitted to retain any shade of their original yellow, they are deficient in beauty, at least to the eye of the connoisseur.

The first step in this part of the process is to procure proper bleaching materials. Many persons are entirely successful in the use of chloride of lime,

3 *   (29)

while others prefer Labarraque's solution of chloride of soda. The former should be prepared for use in the following manner: Take a half pound of strong chloride of lime, and place it in an earthen or other pitcher. Add three pints of soft, cold water, and stir carefully with an iron spoon, pressing so as to mash the lumps well against the sides of the vessel. Keep it covered, and allow it to stand in a cool place until the lime has precipitated upon the bottom of the pitcher, which will be done in about an hour, except a small portion that may remain floating on the surface. This should be removed with a spoon or skimmer, after which the clear liquid should be poured off into a bottle, then corked up tightly, and kept in a cool place.

When ready to commence leaf bleaching, take a glass jar, such as is used for pickles or preserves, having a mouth wide enough to admit the largest leaf. First, select those intended to be whitened, but be careful not to place leaves and seed-vessels in the same jar; then with soft, clear water cover the leaves in the jar, and add the bleaching solution in the proportion of two tablespoonfuls to a pint of water. The jar should be covered tightly, and set in a warm place. When coarse seed-vessels and stems are to be bleached, this proportion of the chloride of lime may be doubled, but the delicate leaves, and especially the Ferns, will be destroyed if the solution be made too strong.

Labarraque's preparation of chloride of soda acts gently and more slowly, and being free from the caustic properties of the lime, is less likely to attack and corrode the delicate framework of the leaves. The quantity of this solution to be added to water, must be double that of the first named preparation. It will whiten the flowers, Ferns, and more tender of the seed-vessels, but it is not strong enough to act on those which are coarser and more ligneous. There is great difficulty, however, in procuring this preparation of the required freshness and strength, as its bleaching properties depend entirely on the amount of chlorine contained in it; and this being a very volatile gas, it is readily lost by keeping a length of time, even when carefully corked and sealed.

The best preparation for this purpose, is that made expressly for use in whitening these skeleton leaves, &c., and may always be had of J. E. Tilton & Co., or their agents. One bottle of this will whiten a large number of leaves, without injuring the fibre, or making them brittle, as is the case with the chloride of lime. The proper proportion for mixing will be about half a

teacupful to a pint of water. This will generally whiten
two sets of leaves; that is, as soon as those first put
in are perfectly white, they may be taken out, and a
second lot placed in the same mixture. Sometimes,
however, it will be necessary to add a small quantity
more, say a tablespoonful, in order to complete them.
For amateurs, and even for accomplished artists, a
superior solution, thus ready prepared to their hands,
will be found safer, and more likely to insure perfect
success, than any preparation they will be able to compound for themselves. The saving of trouble in using
it will be quite a consideration. Had the writer been
able to purchase it, when commencing her labors, it
would have saved her many losses and disappointments. But that so great a help can now be obtained,
affords strong evidence of the advancement of the art
in this country.

In putting the delicate leaves into the jar, care
should be taken to arrange them beforehand with the
stems all pointing the same way, that is, downward
in the jar. The reason for this exists in the fact
that the bleaching commences first at the bottom of
the vessel; and as the thick stems and mid-ribs require
more time to whiten them than the lace-like portion
of the leaves, it insures their being satisfactorily fin-

ished in a short time. A jar of leaves will usually require from six to twelve hours for bleaching; but as the jar is of glass, an outside inspection will enable the operator to judge of the degree of whiteness, without raising the lid until it may be time to remove them.

When they are discovered to be entirely white, they must be taken carefully out with the hand, and laid in a basin of clean, warm water. If suffered to remain too long in the jar, they will become too tender for removal. They may then be thoroughly washed from the chlorine, by changing them several times in fresh water, after which they will be ready for their final drying. This is accomplished as before, by laying them between the folds of a soft towel; while the more delicate ones, which are apt to curl in drying, should now be laid between the leaves of a book, until entirely dry. The washing is a very important part of the operation, as, if not thoroughly done, the bouquet will soon become yellow, and otherwise discolored, and thus, in the end, lose its attractiveness and beauty as a parlor ornament.

As before stated, it will be advisable to keep the seed-vessels separate from the leaves, and to put them in different bleaching jars. If placed promiscuously in the same jar, the seed-vessels will become so entangled in the fine network of the leaves, that in the attempt to remove them the latter will be seriously injured. Seed-vessels and flowers require the same treatment in bleaching and washing, only remembering that the coarser seed-vessels may need a stronger infusion of the bleaching preparation. A little experience will soon inform the operator as to the exact quantity required for all kinds of leaves and seed-vessels.

The bleaching of the Ferns will need some special directions. Many who have succeeded admirably with leaves, have invariably failed in their attempts at preparing these graceful sprays. As they constitute the most brilliant embellishment which can be introduced into a bouquet, such failures are especially mortifying. But by closely following these simple directions, there will be no difficulty in producing entire sprays of white Fern ready to be arranged with other materials for the bouquet.

Having gathered Ferns of different varieties during their season of maturity, — which is when the seeds are to be found on the back of the leaves, — they should be preserved by pressing them between the leaves of a book, there to remain until required for

bleaching. When ready for that process, let the operator select such as she desires, and place them carefully
in a jar, causing them to curl around the sides rather
than with stems downward, in order to avoid breaking
the dry and brittle leaves. The smaller separate leaflets may occupy the space in the centre of the jar.
Then fill up the jar with warm water, leaving room
for the bleaching solution, in the proportion of half a
teacupful of Tilton's preparation to a pint of water.
Cover the jar tightly, and set in a very warm place.
After twenty-four hours, gently pour off the liquid, and
replace with fresh, mixed as before. They should remain in the second water about forty-eight hours, when
this, in like manner, will require to be changed. In
about three or four days the Ferns will begin to whiten
at the edges, and this whiteness will gradually extend
itself over the entire surface of the spray, changing it
from a dark, brownish green to the spotless purity of a
snowflake. Each one must be carefully taken out as
soon as it is seen to be entirely white, without waiting
for the whole contents of the jar to be finished.

In the bleaching of a large spray, it sometimes hap-
pens that its extremity, perhaps half of the entire
length, will become perfectly white, while dark spots
remain on the upper or stem end. In such cases it

will be safest to take out the branch, and, laying it in a basin of water, cut off the white portion, and return the unfinished remainder to the jar. Afterwards, when both are ready for the bouquet, the two portions can be neatly united with gum arabic. The process of changing the water will have to be repeated four or five times during the operation of bleaching the same lot of Ferns, and the time required to whiten them completely will extend over a period of from one to two weeks. The time depends on the varieties of Ferns which may be used, as there is a wide difference in their susceptibilities, some being wholly unfitted for this purpose.

When the sprays are found to be entirely white, they must be taken from the jar with the fingers, always holding them by the stem, and laid in a broad basin of clean, warm water, where they should be allowed to remain for several hours. They may be thoroughly rinsed by changing the water several times, but they will not bear handling in the same manner as will the skeleton leaves. When ready to be dried, take one spray by the stem and lay it in a broad dish or basin of water, allowing it to float on the surface; then pass under it a sheet of unsized white paper, and in this way lift it out of the water. The spray will cling to the paper, and assume its natural shape. Should any of the small side leaves become crooked or overlapped, they may be readily straightened by using the point of a pin to spread them out in proper shape upon the paper. To get rid of the superfluous moisture contained in the latter, lay the sheet first on a soft towel for a few minutes. The towel will absorb most of the excess of water. After that it must be laid between two other sheets of the same unsized white paper, and pressed in a book.

When all the sprays have been thus removed, and committed to the keeping of the book, a heavy weight should be placed on it, in order to insure their drying smoothly. If desirable, the drying may be accelerated by changing them, after a day or two, into another book, or into new portions of the first. When entirely dry, if some of the thinner varieties are found to adhere to the paper, they may be loosened by pressing the thumb nail on the under side of the paper. It is better, however, even after they are thoroughly pressed and dry, to keep them shut up in a book until wanted for the bouquet, as they have a tendency to curl when exposed to the air.

The writer has given directions for the bleaching of Ferns only by the new preparation of Tilton & Co.,

as it has been proved to be the most reliable compound for that purpose. She has fully tested chloride
of lime, and finds it altogether too severe for these
delicate tissues, while the solution of Labarraque is
much slower in its operation — one bottle of the new
preparation being equal in strength to two of the
article last named.

ARRANGING THE BOUQUETS.

 AVING thus completed the different processes required for the production of the
Phantom Bouquet, with boxes well filled
with a complete assortment of white
and perfect leaves, seed-vessels, and flowers, the artist
comes now to the final operation of combining them into
tasteful groups or bouquets, under glass cases or shades.
These will be found indispensable to the permanent
preservation of what otherwise would be a fleeting beauty.
We may suppose that such a shade, of perfectly white
glass, with stand to receive it, has been provided.

The first thing required will be to form a cushion,
either of blue or black velvet, these colors being found

most effectively to contrast with the white group to be placed upon them. The stand, of walnut or enamel, should have a groove upon its surface, inside of the edge, into which the shade will drop freely. Having cut the velvet of the proper size and shape, allowing for the necessary stuffing, the cushion may be prepared by laying raw or carded cotton on the bottom of the stand, raising it rather higher in the centre, and temporarily securing the circular piece of velvet by means of four tacks on the four opposite sides, thus equally dividing the whole into four parts; the edge may then be firmly and neatly fastened around by gluing, and pressing with a blunt-pointed instrument, until it acquires a proper shape, when the tacks may be removed.

The operator will next require some white gum arabic, dissolved in water so as to be very thick; and the first step preparatory to the arrangement will be that of supplying stems to such of the leaves as may have lost them in the process of maceration. For this purpose, some operators use the old stems of other plants which have been bleached expressly for use, as substitutes, while others prefer white wire covered with paper; but after trial of both these expedients, we give the preference to something more simple, and which possesses the additional advantage of being always within reach, as well as being less liable to become discolored by age.

Take the common white crochet spool cotton, and coarse sizes of sewing thread, to be found in every lady's work-basket, and stiffen them by wetting well with gum arabic. When dry and stiff, stems of the required length can be prepared by gumming neatly to the under side of the leaf, allowing the new stem to extend some distance along the central rib or back-bone of the leaf. If done neatly it will be difficult to detect the substitute. These stems can be left about two inches long, which will be sufficient to admit of joining to form branches, &c., and can of course be cut off if found to be too long. Care should be taken to regulate the size of the thread used by the require-ments of the leaf; a large leaf, with thick mid-rib, calling for a thick and substantial stem, while a deli-cate leaf, like the Ivy, needs a finer one.

The Ivy leaf should always, if possible, be grouped so as to form wreaths, as nearly as may be in ac-cordance with its natural habit of growth, the smaller leaves being placed at the end of the spray.

Having prepared the stems, the grouping may be gracefully done (if the bouquet is to be placed under a low, broad shade) by fastening the stems securely,

4 *

with a little of the thick gum, into a hole made in the centre of the cushion, in such a way as to allow them to bend over slightly, using the large leaves of the Magnolia species as a beginning, and filling in with smaller leaves of other varieties. When a taller shade is to be used, this plan will not answer so well, as it is desirable to bring the group higher up, so as to fill the shade. A piece of white silk-wrapped bonnet wire will answer as a foundation, the upper end being covered with a small piece of white wax.

The leaves may then be grouped around the wire, and tied with white sewing cotton, placing the smaller or medium-sized leaves at the top, and adding the larger ones for the middle of the bouquet. These last will then droop over gracefully when the shade is placed over them, and the seed-vessels and Ferns, which are more effective when arranged in groups on the velvet cushion, will be seen plainly through the lace-like curtain. When the central stem of wire has been covered about two thirds of its length, gum the lower end and insert it firmly into the base, having punched an opening through the cushion, reaching down into the wood itself; this will hold it entirely firm. One of the white seed-vessels of the Balsam Apple forms an effective vase-like receptacle, and when used, the wire may be passed through it, before being gummed, into the stand. The group thus fastened should reach, in the centre, to within three inches of the top of the glass, the leaves of course rising higher as they curve upward from the stem. There should now be prepared a few choice sprays, of leaves and seed-vessels, or perhaps a group of Ferns, and fastened into the cavity thus created, so as to crown the whole, and give it an artistic finish.

On no account should large and heavy seed-vessels, or opaque objects, be placed near the top of the bunch. We have seen many specimens made by beginners, in which Stramonium burrs were conspicuous among delicate leaves at the summit of the bouquet. Of course, this manner of arranging them detracts considerably from the light and airy appearance of the whole; and as the burrs soon become discolored, the little original beauty of such productions will soon be gone, the coarse brown burrs becoming an unsightly blemish, which nothing but their removal from the bouquet can repair.

As a general rule, large sprays of Fern look better and wear better, when placed near the bottom, or directly on the velvet, as they are disposed to curl, especially if placed in the bouquet before they are perfectly dry. All delicate seed-vessels, and the beautiful flowers of the Hydrangea, show to great advantage on the raised cushion, while the large leaves occupy the centre of the group. When finished, a piece of chenille around the outer base of the shade will serve the double purpose of ornament and use, as a protection from dust. On no account should the shade be fastened down, as the contraction and expansion caused by changes of temperature will certainly crack the glass if it be glued fast.

Another very pretty style of arrangement is in a frame, under a convex glass, using a background of blue or black velvet. Leaves, flowers, and ferns may be arranged gracefully, with stems downward, as in the ordinary bouquet, and these afterwards concealed by a large seed-vessel of the Balsam Apple or Stramonium. These latter seed-vessels, however beautiful in texture, and ivory-like in effect, are now generally discarded by those who have had several years experience in the art, on account of their tendency to become brown with age. No matter how white and beautiful the leaves may be, the whole effect will be marred by the presence of a single unsightly brown or yellow burr. Some have adopted this style of the frame, but with a flat plate glass, having the whole finished as a table top, made to move on hinges, similar to the *papier-maché* stands, so that when not in use it may stand in a corner in an upright position.

Another and newer style is the black velvet cross, with cushion of the same color round the base, with wreaths or vines of small leaves — the smallest to be had — entwined around it. The effect of this arrangement is admirable, as it shows with great advantage the beautiful leaves of the Ivy, the Deutzia, the Wistaria, the Bignonia, and the Silver Poplar, as they are displayed upon the dark-colored background. A wooden cross, of the height and proportions required, covered neatly with velvet, should be firmly glued into the wooden base, and the white vines formed of the stiffened crochet cotton — the little stems which are to connect the leaves with the vine being made of the finer thread. The exercise of a nice taste, with some little mechanical dexterity, are all that will be required to produce a very happy effect. A few leaves, Ferns, and small seed-vessels, grouped around the base, complete the arrangement.

Still another style, suggested by the desire to transmit specimens of the art by mail or otherwise, to friends at a distance, consists in the grouping in a box, having a dark lining, and gumming the leaves on the bottom of the box, precisely as for framing. The bouquet thus sent can be framed by the receiver by merely cutting off the rim or sides of the box. A deep *passe-partout* frame, made of dark paper, will answer very well for small bouquets. Still other designs, wreaths in vases, albums, &c., will suggest themselves to the proficient in this graceful art; and with accumulated experience will come enlarged ideas of the beautiful, whose further development will soon embellish many a home of taste.

PHANTOM FLOWERS.

ENTWINED AROUND A CROSS.

THEY are spirits of flowers that blossomed and died
Long since in the garden — its beauty and pride ;
Yet they rise from corruption, in robes new and bright,
As vision-like phantoms, all spotless and white.

Gay bodies we knew have gone down to decay ;
With the Winter's first breath they have withered away ;
But a change has come o'er them, and dream-like and fair,
The features that marked them they once again wear.

The same wondrous tissue, the outline and grace
Of each tiny leaflet and blossom we trace,
True type of ourselves, whose poor bodies shall rise
From the grave of corruption, the heirs of the skies.

Dear sign of our hope, of salvation the key,
The purest of offerings thy chaplet shall be ;
Of blossoms unfading, from heavenly bowers,
We twine round the Cross phantom leaflets and flowers.

ILLUSTRATED LIST OF PLANTS FOR SKELETONIZING.

I N describing the process of maceration in a previous chapter, we have endeavored to give such clear and practical directions as will apply to all varieties of plants. But there are certain peculiarities which seem to be inherent in each particular leaf, seed-vessel, and flower, so as to call for specific directions, in order that success may be insured with all. Instead, therefore, of dismissing the subject with a mere list of leaves adapted to the purposes of the art, and leaving each learner to discover these varying peculiarities for herself, at great cost of time and labor, we shall give a few general rules for the treat-

(48)

ment of each one named. The learner will need all
the light that can be thrown on the subject, and the
minute particulars which follow will contribute largely
to her successful prosecution of the art. The illustrations which accompany the description of such leaves
as are most important, will enable the reader to de-
termine the names of doubtful varieties.

MAGNOLIA.

This splendid genus of trees deserves to be placed
at the head of our list of those plants whose leaves
are well adapted to the purposes of our art. Its varied
species are to be found on the eastern shores of both
the great continents North America and Asia. The
United States produces no less than eight varieties,
while China and Japan have four or five. Neither
Europe, Africa, nor South America can offer a single
species of indigenous Magnolia.

The different varieties of Chinese Magnolia have,
with one or two exceptions, been acclimated with us,
and are to be found in most of our ornamental shrub-
beries, their lovely white and purple blossoms and

5

spicy fragrance, together with the neat and regular
appearance of the trees themselves, making them general favorites.   Most of the Chinese varieties will
answer for our purpose, but we give preference to the
following: first, —

WHITE CHINESE MAGNOLIA (*Magnolia conspicua*).

This variety blossoms during April in the Middle
States, and by the Chinese is called the Lily Tree, from
its lily-shaped flowers, of a creamy white color.   The
leaves arrive at perfection in June, and may be gathered for maceration between the 15th of that month
and the middle of September.   After that time the
ravages of insects begin to show themselves.

Magnolia Purpurea and Magnolia Soulangianna are
purple varieties, of Chinese origin, and may be gathered and treated as the above-named.   From four to
six weeks will generally be long enough for their perfect maceration, when they can be readily cleaned by
the aid of warm water and rubbing between the
thumb and finger.

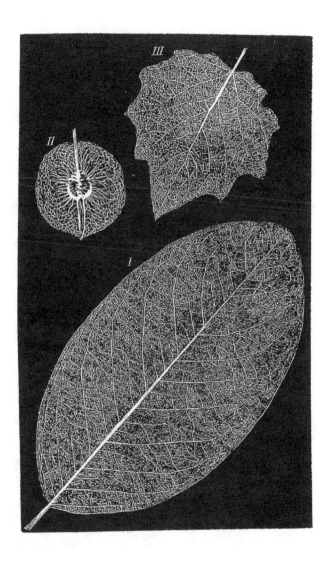

AMERICAN SWAMP MAGNOLIA (*Magnolia glauca*).

(Cut No. 1.)

This is the fragrant wild Magnolia, which blooms in June, and is found in great profusion in the swamps and marshes of New Jersey. When transplanted to the garden, the leaves are produced in great perfection, while their size is increased by cultivation. They are in perfection at the time of blossoming, and on no account should be gathered later, as after that time they become too tough, and abound with invisible stings of insects, whose injuries, not becoming apparent until after the cleansing process has been completed, the otherwise beautiful leaf will be found covered with small black spots, which can neither be whitened nor removed. These leaves require three or four months to macerate, and may then be brushed with a toothbrush to remove the little cellular particles which fill up the interstices, and which give to them a thick and cloudy appearance.

SILVER POPLAR (*Abele*).

(Cut No. 3.)

This leaf is one of the most desirable, as well as most easily cleaned, since it requires but four or five weeks to macerate, and has a strong fibre. The leaves of this tree present much variety of shape, and the sizes of those which are matured vary from half an inch to four inches in length. They may be gathered as early as the 1st of June, and generally remain free from spots until September. Avoid the foliage of the suckers, which are frequently found growing vigorously around the parent tree, as the fibres of such leaves are too weak and tender for our purpose. They will lose their stems by maceration, but these may be replaced, as directed in a previous chapter.

ASPEN POPLAR (*Populus tremula*).

The leaf of this tree is larger than that of the preceding, and is also more delicate. It may be gathered in June or July, and will require about a month to macerate. Great care will be necessary in handling them.

TULIP POPLAR (*Liriodendron tulipifera*).
LOMBARDY POPLAR (*Populus pyramidalis*).

Both these may be gathered early in summer, and should be treated like the Aspen Poplar.

NORWAY MAPLE (*Acer platanoides*).

(Cut No. 4.)

The most beautiful of the Maple family, in shape and general adaptability, to the present purpose. A single branch taken from one of these trees will present great variety in size and shape, the small leaves at the extremities cleaning quite as perfectly as the largest. They should be gathered by the 20th of June, certainly not later than the middle of July. They will be finished in about six weeks, losing their stems, as is invariably the case with all the Maples. The Silver Maple may be treated by the same rule.

LINDENS AND WEEPING WILLOWS.

(Cut No. 16. Willow.)

These two desirable leaves may be gathered in July, and will macerate in from six weeks to two months. They need very careful handling, or brushing with a camel's hair brush on a plate.

EUROPEAN SYCAMORE (*Acer pseudo-platanus*).

(Cut No. 6.)

A beautiful leaf, in shape somewhat resembling the Norway Maple, but possessing a firmer and thicker

5 *

texture. It must be secured early in June, as by the close of that month it becomes unfitted for our use, and but few of those collected after the 20th of June will come out entirely free from clouds or blemishes. About two months will complete their maceration.

Ash.

(Cut No. 5. English Ash.)

There are several species of this family which are admirably adapted for our object. Of these, the Flowering Ash (*Ornus Europœus*) and the English Ash are the most beautiful. They will become clear and perfectly skeletonized in about six weeks after gathering, which may be done in July and August.

Everlasting Pea, or Chichling Vetch (*Lathyrus*).

(Cut No. 11.)

This pretty garden perennial, with an abundance of deep pink blossoms, is too well known to need description. The leaves may be gathered at any time during summer, and require but a few weeks for maceration. They lose their stems. The graceful tendrils of this vine may also be placed in water with the leaves,

and after remaining some weeks, the outer cuticle can be easily removed without untwisting the curl, and these, when bleached, will be found ornamental to the bouquet, especially where the design adopted consists of a vine.

Elm.

The leaves of this beautiful tree must be gathered very early. Indeed, so soon do the caterpillars begin their ravages, that in some sections of the country, before the leaf is strong enough for the purpose of the skeletonizer, it is too much eaten to be worth collecting. June or July will answer, if any perfect leaves are then to be found. They will macerate in about four weeks, and being very delicate, will need the greatest care. If the leaf be laid on a plate, or something similar, a camel's hair pencil will remove the softened particles, leaving the fibre clean, to be floated off into the basin of water, and then laid carefully on a towel to dry.

The Evergreen Elm (*Ulmus sempervipens*) (Cut No. 8), is a small, glossy leaf, with scalloped edges, and may be used at any season of the year, requiring about three months for its perfect clearing. A native of France, and is rare in America.

DEUTZIA SCABRA, OR ROUGH-LEAVED DEUTZIA.

(Cut No. 8.)

One of the most beautiful small leaves we can use. Gather them in June and July. They will be perfectly skeletonized in three or four weeks, without losing their stems. These graceful little leaves, with serrated edges, form beautiful wreaths and sprays, either for black velvet crosses, or to be twined around the base of a bouquet.

Deutzia Gracilis, another variety of this desirable garden plant, requires somewhat longer for its perfect preparation.

BEACH, HICKORY, AND CHESTNUT.

These leaves contain a slight portion of tannin, and had better be kept separate from other kinds. A few drops of muriatic acid added to the water in which they are placed for maceration, will hasten the process. They may be gathered in July, and will require several months to become completely skeletonized.

DWARF PEAR, SASSAFRAS, AND ALTHEA

(Cut No. 9.)

Gather in July. They require about two months.

Rose.

(Cut No. 7.)

The common annual blooming dark velvet Rose furnishes the best description of leaves for our purpose. They should be gathered in July before the insects have stung them, and will require about two months' soaking. They are very delicate, and must be brushed on a plate.

White Fringe Tree (*Chionanthus Virginica*).

Gather in July. Will be ready for clearing in about two months.

Dutchman's Pipe (*Aristolochia tomentosa*).

This is a rather coarse vine, of rank growth, well suited for covering unsightly buildings or decaying trees. It bears a curious white blossom, shaped somewhat like a pipe, whence it takes its homely name. The leaves are heart-shape, of thick and woolly texture, but the skeletons they produce are so exceedingly beautiful as to make them indispensable to a complete collection. They should be taken from the vine not earlier than the middle of July, and perfect specimens may be obtained as late as the middle of September, — probably about the first of August will be the best time. Select the firmest and oldest leaves. Some of them will be clear in four weeks after immersion.

Ivy.

(Cut No. 17.)

These much admired leaves may be gathered at any time during the year, always selecting those a year old in preference to the younger growth of the present season. The Ivy leaf, like some others, has a tough outer cuticle on each side, between which the fibrous skeleton is concealed, the intermediate space being filled with the green cellular matter common to all leaves. During the process of maceration this green substance becomes dissolved, though the outer skin remains whole and entire. When taken from the macerating vessel and laid in the clean water for cleansing, this skin will present the appearance of a bladder filled with green water. By puncturing, or gently tearing this skin on one or both

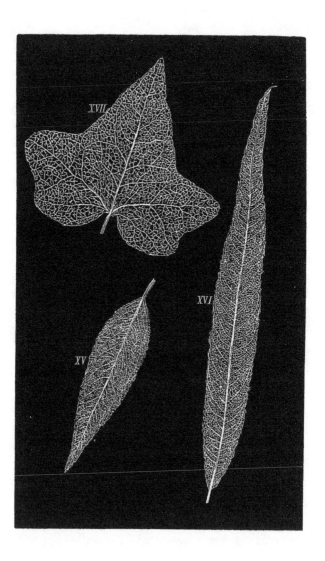

sides of the leaf, the water will escape, and the perfect skeleton will float out, ready for rinsing and drying. Four or five weeks will be sufficient to allow for their preparation, although some varieties require a few weeks longer.

HOLLY.

(Cut. No. 12.)

This leaf is quite difficult to clear properly, owing to the tough outer cuticle adhering so tenaciously to the thorns on the edges, as to tax the ingenuity and patience of the operator in removing the one without breaking off the other. For this reason most amateurs give up after the first attempt, and content themselves with more beautiful and less troublesome subjects. About three months is the time necessary for skeletonizing them; and being evergreens, they may be gathered at any time.

Wistaria, Bignonia, Greenbrier, and Wild Yam, all vines that are tolerably well known, may be skeletonized by the usual process in from six weeks to three months, and should be gathered about the middle of July.

Of greenhouse plants, the leaves of Camellia Japonica, Cape Jasmine, Laurestina, and Caoutchouc may

be done after months of soaking. A shorter process,
however, which some parties prefer for all descriptions
of leaves to the slower method which we have adopted,
is found to answer well for these particular species.
Their tough epidermis requires something more than
the ordinary sluggish operation of water and summer
heat to soften and remove them. The process consists in boiling them for several hours in strong soap-
suds, using the ordinary chemical soap of the shops.

This will generally succeed with these last named
plants, but for those which are tender and delicate, as
before described, it is too severe. Besides this, the
chemical properties of the soap affect the leaf in so
peculiar a way as to increase the difficulty of bleaching; and notwithstanding all possible care be taken
to wash after the boiling process is over, enough of
the refractory element remains to defeat all attempts
to make the leaf perfectly and permanently white.
Therefore, while we mention the process, as an item
of information due to the learner who desires to
understand the whole routine, and to test for herself
the various modifications of practice now in use, yet
we prefer and still adhere to our own formula, as at
first described. We consider it the best, and by far
the most reliable, although it is unquestionably slow

and tedious in all its various processes. Our motto in this art must be " Festina lente."

In concluding our list of these, the most desirable leaves that have so far come under our own observation, we would by no means limit the researches and experiments of other artists. Different localities will unquestionably furnish different specimens, and thus their collections may be greatly enlarged by the adoption of new and more beautiful leaves. As a general rule to govern in the selection of appropriate subjects for experiment, let those of strong and woody fibre be chosen, rather than thick, fleshy leaves, whose veins or ribs may be soft and juicy. Avoid, also, those which have veins traversing the leaf in a longitudinal direction, instead of forming a network tissue radiating from the mid-rib to the outer edges of the leaf. The former are known as endogenous, the latter as exogenous varieties of leaf structure. As an example of the endogenous, we may cite the leaves of different kinds of Lilies. If put into the macerating vessel, a few days, or a week, will be sufficient to reduce them to a mass of pulp, resembling a bunch of thread or strings, with apparently no connecting framework to hold the fibres together in form. The practised eye can in most cases discover the character of the leaf

6

under observation, by merely holding it up against the light, when the veinwork will be plainly perceptible, and its value decided by the closeness or coarseness of its vascular structure.

We add the following, as having been successfully skeletonized : —

Horse Chestnut (*Æsculus hippocastanum*).

Kentucky Coffee Tree (*Ginnocladus Canadensis*).

Flowering Pear (*Pyrus Japonica*).

Andromeda.

Rose Acacia (*Robinia hispida*).

Witch Hazel (*Hamamelis Virginica*), said to be very beautiful, — should be gathered early.

Wild Cherry (*Cerasus serotina*).

Sugar Berry (*Celtis occidentalis*).

Fraxinella Dictamnus.

Franciscea, — very beautiful.

Erythrina Crystigalla.

Virgilia Lutea.

Matronia.

Barberry (*Berberis aristata*, and *purpurea*).

Mountain Laurel (*Rhododendron*).

Box.

Butcher's Broom (*Ruscus hypophyllum*).

SEED–VESSELS.

IFFERENT varieties of the Ground Cherry family (*Physalis*) are entitled to particular notice. The peculiar characteristic of this family of plants is the berry, enclosed in a bladder-like receptacle. These berries are about the size of cherries, with color yellow, red, or purple, and having a pleasant, sweet taste. The green covering becomes of a yellowish color when the fruit is ripe, and they fall to the ground together, when the curious case will soon become perfectly skeletonized by contact with the damp ground. But as they are very liable to be eaten by insects while on the ground, it is much better to gather them as soon as they fall, and place them in the macerating vessel, allowing the berry inside to remain until softened, in order to avoid tearing the delicate little bladder. Two or three weeks will be sufficiently long to allow for their preparation. They may be washed, by passing rapidly to and fro in hot water, when the softened berry may be pressed out, then dried with a soft towel. Some species lose their stems, and may be prepared for the bouquet by using the gummed thread, being careful to bend gracefully, so as to give the effect of drooping.

WILD HOP *Ptelia trifoliata*).
(Cut No. 2.)

This is a membranous capsule surrounded by a leafy border, which, after about two weeks' soaking, becomes very lace-like and beautiful. Before bleaching, the seed may be removed by making an incision on one side of the capsule, being careful, when afterwards arranging it, to place that side downwards.

NICANDRA PHYSALOIDES.

One of the most desirable and showy for this purpose. The blue Nicandra should be cultivated by all makers of the Phantom Bouquet. The calyx of the plant, enclosing first the flower, and afterwards the seed capsule, is of a curious balloon shape, of bright green until the seed is ripe, when it becomes brownish. Each one has a tough stem, which is retained through maceration, and is attached to the stalk of the plant, the latter being covered by the calyxes, at a distance of an inch apart, quite to the end of the branch. This calyx seems to be formed of five distinct divisions, like leaves, which, when pressed open and bent in proper shape, has, after bleaching, every appearance of a flower. To increase the variety in the bouquet, they can be used both in their natural form to represent buds, or in the way described. They require about three weeks to macerate, when they may be cleaned in hot water, aided perhaps by the tooth-brush. A whole branch may be done without separating from the main stem.

THORN APPLE : JAMESTOWN WEED (*Datura Stramonium*).

A well known rank wayside weed, very poisonous to the taste, but not to the touch. The seed-vessels should be gathered when ripe, and soaked about six weeks, when, by aid of a stiff brush, the beautiful skeleton will appear. When bleached, they resemble carved ivory, and are much admired in the bouquet. The only drawback to their value is their tendency to become brown again after bleaching. For this cause we have entirely discarded them.

WILD CUCUMBER, OR BALSAM APPLE (*Echinosystis*).

This is one of the most curious specimens in our list of beautiful seed-vessels. It is said to grow in abundance in the neighborhood of Boston, bearing a profusion of seed. The seed-vessels vary in size from an inch to nearly two inches in length, and about half that in thickness. They become perfect skeletons on the vine, where they should be allowed to remain until the frost has opened them and dropped the seed. If not entirely clear when gathered, they may be completed by a few weeks' soaking. They form beautiful vase-like receptacles for the base of the bouquet, and as they retain their whiteness, are excellent substitutes for the Stramonium burrs.

LOBELIA.

The little wild species is very beautiful, with its delicate globes set along the stem. About three weeks will do for them, when they will become clear by passing to and fro in a basin of hot water.

SKULL CAP (*Scutellaria*).

These delicate clusters of seed-vessels may be skeletonized in two or three weeks, and cleared in the same way as the Lobelia.

SHELL-FLOWER (*Phyton Concha*).

A curious shell-shaped calyx, with four seeds, which remain in the extreme point of the horn. The plant is rare, and rather difficult to cultivate. It seems to belong to the Sage family, and has an aromatic odor when pressed. The calyx is very delicate, and will macerate in ten days or less. When seen in a group of Phantom Leaves, they somewhat resemble the Convolvulus blossom.

POPPY.

The cultivated garden varieties will macerate in a week or two. The fibre does not remain very perfect, at least in a general way, as it is apt to tear by removal of the inner skins. But the star-shaped summit of the capsule looks well upon the velvet cushion. The black lines which radiate from the centre may be removed by aid of a pin, when a beautiful lace-work appearance will be imparted to it.

MALLOWS.

Several varieties. The common garden Mallows, with calyx enclosing seeds, are the prettiest. They grow in clusters, and if suffered to remain until frost, will become skeletonized on the plant.

HYDRANGEA HORTENSIA.

(Cut No. 13.)

The well known garden species — the bunches should be left on the plant until late in September, in order to become firm. Separate into small bunches, leaving not more than four or five in a cluster. They will require about ten or twelve weeks for maceration, and may then be cleansed by passing to and fro in hot water, changing the water frequently as it becomes filled with the loose particles. If some of the leaves are separated, they can easily be re-placed after bleaching by gum arabic.

HYDRANGEA QUERCIFOLIA : OAK-LEAVED HYDRANGEA.

(Cut No. 14.)

This is a tougher and coarser species, composed of four flat petals. It requires longer time to macerate than the Hydrangea Hortensia, but should be gathered as soon as the bunches begin to turn brown on the tree. A brush will be necessary to clear properly.

CAMPANULA.

The seed-vessels of the several species of these, including the Canterbury Bell, are much admired in the bouquet, although not so delicate as the Lobelia, which they resemble. Some varieties will become sufficiently prepared on the plant, and only require bleaching, but others need two or three weeks' maceration.

To the above list the following may be added :

Black Henbane (*Hyoscyamus niger*).
English Monkshood (*Aconitum Napellus*).
Toad Flax (*Colutea arborescens*).
Wild Salvia.
Figwort (*Scrophularia nodosa*).

Jerusalem Cherry (*Solanum pseudo-capsicum*).
Bladder Nut (*Staphylea trifolia*)
Safflower: False Saffron (*Carthamus tinctoria*).
False Pennyroyal (*Isanthus cerula*).
Lily of the Valley: The dried Flowers.

In concluding these instructions in the art of preparing and completing the Phantom Bouquet, we have
endeavored to be plain and practical in every particular, seeking not only to direct the learner in her
experiments, but also to guard her against the mis-
takes and disappointments which must invariably attend
the labors of the unassisted amateur. If the details
here given have appeared minute and tedious, let the
reader remember that in these very trifles consist
the true elements of success.

When the first bouquets appeared for sale in this
country, the admiration they excited awakened a general curiosity as to the process by which they were
produced. Inquiries were addressed to the editors
of some of our scientific journals, but they could
answer only according to their own very limited
knowledge of the art ; and hence this occasional
information was exceedingly vague and unreliable,
and, indeed, it often misled the learner, resulting in

discouragement to some, and in entire disgust to others.

The writer has here given her own practical rules and ideas, adopted from actual experience, and no careful learner need hesitate to follow in her footsteps. But, however invaluable instruction may be to the beginner, personal experiment will be found indispensable. We cannot write up the amateur to the position of an artist. Yet a desire to reach the status of the latter will stimulate to exertion and perseverance, and these, with ordinary taste and skill, will surely be rewarded with success. None, therefore, whose love for the truly beautiful in art is deep and strong, and whose aspirations for eminence are decided and sincere, will permit a few early discouragements to turn them aside from the undertaking.

THE WONDERS AND USES OF A LEAF.

S intimated in a preceding chapter, the prosecution of this new study by one whose attention had never been directed to botanical investigations, will unfold a world of novelties to which she had heretofore been a stranger. She will insensibly become a botanist. The leaves becoming her peculiar study, she will be surprised by the discovery of peculiarities, and charmed by the revelation of beauties, which she did not imagine as existing in the leafy world. From a desire to extend her knowledge of the subject, she will consult the numerous botanical authorities which crowd the shelves of the nearest library, and thus her interest in a study so elevating and refining, will be increased. From these she will learn a multitude of facts, such as nothing short of the most elaborate chemical analysis could have detected, some of which will be found peculiarly relevant to the study in hand.

It would be out of place to crowd these pages with extended extracts from botanical authorities ; but a brief summary from some of them, in relation to the structure and functions of a leaf, will be quite appropriate. All plants, in a general sense, receive their food in a soluble state, through their roots. The tree receives its supply of minerals, such as silex, lime, alumina, potassa, and magnesia, also in solution. The sap, thus charged with nourishment, ascends the trunk, traverses the branches, and passes into the leaf. The superflous water, which held the nourishment in solution, passes off by perspiration from the leaf, but the plant refuses to part with the nourishment contained in the water. This is distributed throughout the plant, a portion being deposited in the cells of the leaf. The wonderful plexus of minute vessels which traverses its whole cellular tissue becomes clogged as the season advances, its circulating functions gradually cease to operate, and long before winter they are wholly suspended. The

7

leaf loses its hold on the parent spray, and finally falls to the ground.

Chemistry has proved that at this period it contains a large amount of mineral matter. The autumnal leaf contains a much larger proportion than when it was young and succulent; hence the facility of maceration in summer, and the impossibility of doing so in autumn. It is a remarkable fact that the leaf contains a larger proportion of mineral matter than the body of the tree. Thus, the dried leaves of the Elm contain more than eleven per cent. of earthy matter, while the wood contains less than two per cent. The Beech, the Willow, the Pitch Pine, and other trees, present differences almost as great.

One of the most remarkable properties of the leaves is their power of decomposing carbonic acid, thus enabling them to contribute, in common with the roots, to the growth of the plant. The largest part of all plants consists of carbon and the elements of water. The woody fibre is formed of carbon, hence the growth and increase of all trees and plants are dependent on their capacity for taking up and digesting this substance. But they neither find it nor take it up in a free or simple state, but in the form of carbonic acid, that is, carbon combined with oxygen. This carbonic acid pervades the atmosphere, from which the leaves are constantly separating it from the oxygen, and appropriating its carbon as a continuous contribution to the growth of the plant. The roots, by a process of their own, in like manner extract the same substance from the carbonic acid of the water around and below them, and convey it upward into the body of the plant. But much the largest portion of the carbonic acid which forms the food of plants, is absorbed by the leaves.

As carbon, and not carbonic acid, is the food of plants, the power of decomposing the latter, so as to leave them in possession of the former, and of expelling the superfluous oxygen, is therefore indispensable to their growth. In reality, the leaves are the lungs, as their functions are strikingly analogous to those performed by the lungs of animals. The green leaves of a growing plant absorb carbonic acid; they expose it to the action of the sun's light ; the oxygen is separated from the carbonic acid, and is given out by the leaves ; the carbon remains, and, entering into the system of the plant, immediately increases its bulk.

The growth and vigor of the tree depend on the rapidity with which this decomposition, or digestion of carbonic acid, goes on. The leaves must not only be exposed to the light, but their color must be green. Such plants as have been grown in the dark are invariably feeble and destitute of strength and substance, but they are also without color. This is owing to the deficiency of carbon ; for while they may absorb carbonic acid from the air, the absence of sunshine prevents them from separating it. When the leaves lose their natural green color, it is evidence of disease. The plant has in great measure lost its power of digesting its food, and remedies must be resorted to to remove the cause. The books abound in instances of all descriptions of plants being thus affected, while the remedial agencies are happily quite as numerous, and in many cases entirely successful.

Such are the powers of absorption possessed by the leaves. Their capacity for giving off exhalations are equally wonderful. Botanists have carefully measured the extent of this exhalation in certain plants. An Apple-tree, with twelve square feet of foliage, perspires nine ounces of water per day. A Vine of similar dimensions exhaled from five to six ounces daily. A Sunflower, three and a half feet high, was found to perspire at the rate of twenty to thirty ounces of moisture every twelve hours, or seventeen times more than a man.

These facts prove that the greater portion of the crude liquids which are taken up by the roots of a plant, passes off into the atmosphere through the leaves. The quantity of moisture thus appropriated by some plants must be enormous, as the foregoing experiments with small ones sufficiently prove. Large trees, presenting a great expanse of foliage, must necessarily exhale immense amounts of moisture. Thus, forest lands which are wet, and even swampy, become dry on being cleared. Gardens which are unduly crowded, are generally damp from the copious exhalations proceeding from excessive foliage. From the same cause proceeds the dampness in houses whose exterior is enveloped by shrubs or running vines.

From the large proportion of mineral matter contained in the leaves, it is evident that the same substances existing in the earth must be annually circulating from one to the other. The roots extract them from the soil, they ascend the tree with the sap, and are deposited in the leaves. Having given them coherency and strength, and having probably performed other functions which are yet unknown to either botanist or chemist, the fall and decay of the leaves

7*

returns these mineral ingredients to the earth. With
the succeeding year the mysterious circuit is repeated,
the tree enlarging in bulk, and the forest soil increasing in richness. Such forest soils, instead of being
impoverished by the growth of trees, receive back annually the greater portion of those mineral elements
necessary to the tree, with much organic matter received into the plant from the atmosphere. The roots
suck up these minerals from great depths, but the
leaves deposit them on the surface. The surface soils
are therefore gaining instead of losing.

These annual deposits of leaves upon a forest soil
are indispensable to the vigor of the trees. If, for
neatness' sake, the owner of a park or grove should
sweep away the autumnal deposit, and continue to do
so for a term of years, he would ultimately remove
so large a quantity of mineral matter as to impov-
erish the ground, and greatly check the growth of
the trees. It is because of the peculiar deposits found
in all leaves, that leaf manure is prized so highly by
every intelligent gardener. While generally regarded
as a purely vegetable substance, leaves are perhaps
the best mineral manure that can be applied to the
soil. It is alleged, moreover, on very high authority,
that the most efficient manure for any plant is found

in the decomposed leaves and trimmings of its own species.

The science which enables us to understand not only the history, the names, the virtues, and the associations connected with all plants, as well as the wonderful relations, the admirable laws which govern their structure, and the important part they bear in the economy of the universe, is worthy of the careful study of every intelligent person. He will find it worth while to become familiar with a science which, wherever his steps may lead him, from the bleak mountain-top, crusted over with mosses and lichens only, to warm and luxuriant tropical valleys, where the magnificence of vegetable wonders almost bewilders the senses, will still furnish him with new subjects for admiration. It will make his morning walk in the garden or over the meadow a new delight. A tramp along the commonest field path, or a ramble by the wayside, which, to the eye of the dull and unlearned, may be mean and barren, he will find rich in interest and exuberant in beauty. No thinking person, whose home is in the country, and who loves Nature, would fail to find in such studies an inexhaustible fund of gratification. The fields, the forests, the entire landscape have a positively different and altogether new meaning to one who sees, not only the general beauty of the whole display, but who also studies with delight every detail of fern, or shrub, or forest tree in the foreground.

LEAF PRINTING.

T will sometimes be desirable to make impressions of the skeletonized leaves, either for preservation as curiosities in the scrap book or photographic album, for transmission by mail as specimens of the art, or for the engraver to reproduce on wood. The making of these impressions, direct from the leaves, though an exceedingly simple process when once understood, requires much care and skill to learn. Whoever may undertake to produce them, should call in, if possible, the aid of some friend who has a practical knowledge of printing, as the processes by which books and newspapers are produced are all applicable to leaf printing.

The operator should procure a spoonful of printer's ink, and with a case knife spread a small quantity over half the surface of a marble slab about a foot square. When spreading the ink on the slab, let it be confined to one end of it, not letting it cover more than half the stone. Care must be taken not to allow thick streaks or ridges of ink, but to spread a thin film or covering, as uniform as possible. As printing ink is a thick and paste-like compound, which stiffens in cold weather, if the operation is to be performed when the temperature is low, the stone should be slightly warmed before the ink is laid on. The warmth will render the ink sufficiently fluid to operate in a satisfactory manner. If no marble slab can be conveniently obtained, then a smooth board, about an inch thick, may be substituted. The board will not require to be warmed.

When the stone has been supplied with ink as above directed, a roller is passed several times over it, until the whole surface of the roller becomes coated. It will take up the ink in unequal quantities, that is, more in one place than in another, with just as much irregularity as it had been laid upon the stone with the knife. This irregularity must now be remedied, and the ink distributed over the entire surface of the roller with absolute uniformity. This is quickly accomplished by frequently passing the roller to and fro over that half of the stone on which no ink had been spread. But in so doing, care must be taken to occasionally lift it from the stone, and to give it a half revolution before again putting it down, so that its surface shall come in contact with new portions of the surface of the stone. By following these directions the ink will become distributed evenly over the face of the roller, whence it will be transferred with corresponding uniformity to the delicate framework of the leaf, and will produce a perfect impression of its most complex veinwork. If the ink is not thus nicely distributed on the roller, the interstices in the leafy structure will become filled with it, and the impression will present an unsightly blotch.

For taking impressions, thin letter paper will be found the best, if it be nicely glazed and free from ridges or water-marks. It should first be cut into pieces about the desired sizes, and then slightly sprinkled with clean water, say two or three pieces first. On these as many dry ones should be laid, and they sprinkled in turn, then more dry ones, then another sprinkling, and so on until the whole quantity has been sprinkled. Let the pile lie for half an hour, or until the paper has absorbed all the water. Then take the pieces, one at a time, and turn them over, placing the first on a board, and the others on top of the first, but shifting them about as they are turned; that is, if a very wet end or corner is observed in one piece, turn the piece around, so that the excessively wet places shall come in contact with dryer surfaces in the new pile. Be particular to smooth all wrinkles with the back of the thumb nail. If the paper has been made too wet, the accident can be remedied by interposing dry pieces between two wet ones. When the whole has been turned, put a slight weight on the pile to press all down smooth, as much depends on having the paper in perfect order.

Being now ready to commence the printing, a leaf is placed on a smooth board, with its under side uppermost, as there the leafy veins or ribs are more prominent than on the upper side. The roller having been charged with ink, it is rolled to and fro over the leaf until the latter is seen to have received a sufficient supply. Three or four times going over will generally be enough. Then lay the leaf on the top sheet of the damp paper pile, with the inked side down, and over it place a doubled sheet of dry paper, press on with the left hand so tight that the leaf shall not move, and with the thumb nail of the right hand rub pretty hard over the whole leaf. This pressure of the thumb nail will transfer the ink on the leaf to the surface of the damp paper, and if the inking has been carefully done, a clear and distinct impression will be obtained. If duplicates are desired, repeat the operation. If the impression is not entirely satisfactory, then try one from the upper surface of the leaf. The printed sheet should be immediately placed between the leaves of a thick book, there to remain until dry, when it will come out nicely pressed, and smooth as before being dampened.

The best form of roller is made by taking a piece of india-rubber hose, say an inch or two in diameter, about five inches long, and forcing it over a round stick, leaving handles projecting at the ends. If the surface of the rubber is very uneven, it should be made uniform by covering it with thick buckskin. Where the rubber hose cannot be readily obtained, a covering for the stick may be made by winding round it several thicknesses of cloth or flannel, and covering it with buckskin. When done printing, the ink should be washed from both stone and roller by turpentine, ley, or strong soap-suds.

Failure in the first attempts should not discourage

8

the operator. The process is a very simple and easy one, and a few trials will generally insure success. All the impressions contained in this volume were taken for the engraver by the process described above. None but the most perfect leaves should be used, as any blemish will be reproduced in the impression.

COMMERCIAL VALUE OF THE ART.

HEN a novelty in science, art, or manufactures becomes the candidate for public favor, the first consideration with the many is, — Will it pay ? With American minds especially, this is the controlling idea. An art is esteemed valuable in proportion to its power of enriching the discoverer. The benefit or pleasure it may confer on the community is a secondary matter, as men usually make new discoveries for their own exclusive gain. Whatever share the public may receive is incidental, but even then they are required to pay for it. The invention of a new machine is valuable to the originator, not

(87)

because the community is to be benefited, but because
it will be compelled to purchase largely. So also
with all processes throughout the range of human
wants. Each has its salable or commercial value.
But few inventors or philosophers originate or discover
solely for the public good.

Applying these tests to the art we have illustrated,
it would seem evident that it is wholly deficient in
commercial value. As an invention, it is not new.
As the common grain fan had been used for ages
in China, before the Dutch discovered it and transplanted it to their own country, whence it was subsequently domesticated here, so the art of skeletonizing flowers had existed in Asia for centuries before
it became known in Europe. Like what is yet known
as the Dutch fan, which no sooner reached this
country than American ingenuity transformed it from
a sluggish and imperfect crudity into a rapid and
efficient machine, so this art, under the touch of
American taste and shrewdness, has been made to
take high rank among the most beautiful creations
of genius. But here the parallel ceases. Fans can
be manufactured by machinery, and every farmer
who produces grain must have one. They are arti-
cles of necessity, not of luxury. Though there be

a limit to their consumption, yet the consumption is nevertheless large enough to give to the article a great commercial value.

But machinery cannot be applied to the production of these delicate tissues. Their preparation is essentially an art, not a manufacture. Like the chiselling of a statue, which must be done by the slow labor of the artist himself, so can their beauties be unveiled only by the most skilful hands. The statuary may employ an ordinary workman to hew away the superfluous mass beneath which lies concealed the graceful creation of his genius, but it is doubtful if a journeyman skeletonizer could be trusted with a single department of the process. The artist must depend more entirely on herself than even the statuary. Hence, a manufacture which will not admit of the aid of machinery, and which is so peculiarly delicate as to exclude that of even human assistance, can have no commercial value. Extensive production is impossible. The world may be readily supplied with grain fans, but a corresponding abundance of skeleton flowers, were there a proportionate demand for them, is beyond the reach of even American ingenuity. Could they have been as rapidly duplicated as apple-parers or nut crackers, they would have long since ceased to be a novelty.

Neither is universal adoption the gauge by which all merits are to be estimated. As the contemplation of an exquisitely chiselled statue will stimulate high and noble thoughts, such as refine the heart and awaken in it new and lofty aspirations, so do all other works of genuine art, no matter to what department they may belong. The present century has shown us that all art is progressive, and that between its progress and the advance of a generally refined taste, there is a parallelism too distinct to be overlooked. The production of a skeletonized flower is one contribution to the general sum of advancement. The flower may be less imposing than the statue, or the canvas, but it is a far more elaborate marvel, combining in a single subject a revelation of the wonders of the Divine Hand so intricate, yet so harmonious, that the chisel of the statuary or the pencil of the painter might seek in vain to rival it. The advent of this should therefore be hailed as a new star in the galaxy. It will contribute its full share to the general fund of innocent and rational gratification. Taste will appreciate its productions, genius will consecrate them, and the devout will cherish them as affording new incentives for veneration.

The art is one which seems designed for female

hands exclusively. If some of its attendant operations are unpleasant, all are yet delicate and gentle. No rude hand can manipulate these tender fibres but to destroy them. As an equivalent for deficient commercial value, their production will afford employment to minds which cannot fail to be thus informed, invigorated, and enlarged. Every where the effect will be to elevate and refine. Should the study be found difficult and abounding with disappointments, it will teach the learner perseverance. If it have its discouragements, it will be found to have its gratifications also. Success in such an art will be worth achieving; and few will be found so selfish as not to be proud of seeing that their friends have conquered it. Commercial value is evidently a most imperfect standard of merit.

The subjoined poetical tributes to the art have been kindly sent to us as appropriate to this volume. The second poem is now published for the first time.

PRESERVED FLOWERS.

HE preservation of Flowers, in their natural forms and colors, is an entirely new article of trade that has arisen in Germany. Erfurt, the city of nurserymen and florists, excels in manufacturing bouquets, wreaths, floral decorations for rooms, dinner tables, etc., made of such flowers. We are glad that we are enabled to lay before our readers the *modus operandi*, by translating for them the following article from the *Deutsches Magazin fur Garten und Blumenkunde*.

First condition : get a lot of fine sand, wash it till all the soluble particles are gone — you can test it

(92)

by pouring the water off till it looks quite clear; when you are quite sure of the fact, pour the sand on stones or boards placed aslant, so that the water can run off, and let it get dry either by sun or fire — dry, perfectly dry. Then pass the sand through a sieve, so that all dusty particles disappear from it, as there will be such, which washing and drying will not have removed. Then pass through a coarse sieve, so as to get rid of too large grains. When that is done, your sand should be a mass of fine particles, of nearly equal size, as is, for instance, the so-called silver sand, used for writing. Keep the sand in a very dry, if possible, also, in a warm place, that no vitalizing quality may remain in it.

Now for the flowers: cut them in a fully developed state, taking care that they are neither wet nor moist by dew, rain, etc. If you cannot obtain them in any other condition, which is to be regretted, then the following troublesome proceeding will render them dry. Take one or two flowers at a time and put them into a glass, into which pour just enough water that the ends can stand in it; the flower will then dry, and still suck up water enough not to fade.

Next, get a box or pot, or any thing large enough to receive your flower or flowers; pour sand enough

into it that they will stand by themselves, their
stems embedded in the sand. And now for that job,
which calls upon your whole skill and your most
delicate fingering; don't be afraid; though practice
renders that, too, a comparatively easy matter. You
have to fill up the box above the level of the flowers
with sand, so that the flowers are completely embedded
in it. By means of a tube, or a funnel, or a sieve,
just accordingly, you can do it in such a way that
every particle of the flower rests in sand, and that
your filling up shall not have crumpled or displaced
the smallest petal. Of course, such a thing can be
done only in a very slow way by a beginner.

And now take care not to shake your box, else
the flower inside might get hurt. Carry it to a
place both dry and warm, that all the moisture in
the flower may pass into the sand, which, being
porous, is in turn acted upon, and will let the
moisture pass entirely out and get evaporated. Avoid,
however, positive heat, or the colors of the flower
will fade; whilst at too low a temperature, the
moisture in the flower will not dry quickly enough,
and so rot it. The warmth should, as a general
thing, never exceed one hundred degrees.

When you are sure that your flowers have fully dried, — a thing a very little practice in touching the box will teach you, — the thing is done. Open the box, and by holding it in a slanting direction, let so much sand run out that you can lift the flower by the stem; by turning it upside down, shaking it gently, and if necessary, blowing on it, all the sand will be removed, and you have the flower in its most perfect form. A little brittle, to be sure, in such a dry state as this, and therefore requiring careful handling. But a few days' exposure to the atmosphere will have imparted moisture enough to the flower to make it considerably less brittle.

You now see why we cannot do with the larger grains of sand; they would press unequally, and spoil the flower, which forever retains all the marks of such pressure; nor with the dusty particles of the sand, because they, as well as the soluble particles which we have removed by washing, would adhere to the hairy and velvety parts of the flower, would never be got rid of, and would materially impair the original beauty.

For the same reason, glabrous flowers are not fit " subjects." The very newest feature, however,

about this business, is, that this discovery, how to
preserve flowers in their natural state, is quite an
old affair, long forgotten, and solely resuscitated by
the increasing demand for bouquets.

APPENDIX

*Although they are not a part of the original book,
we have included the following simple methods for
skeletonizing leaves.*

Method 1 - The Long Soak
(This method does not include the bleaching of leaves.)

Place fresh mature leaves in a large pot or bucket. Fill the
container with water and weigh down the leaves to keep
them submerged. (A folded newspaper set in the water
will weigh enough to keep the leaves submerged without
crushing them.) The container should be stored in a **warm**
place. Any warm out-building or garage is best, since
there is some smell when the tissues start to break down.

After a period of 3 to 4 weeks, rinse leaves under running
water while rubbing the sides gently with your fingers to
completely remove the soft tissue. (If the tissue is not
easily removed, submerge the leaves in water again for
another week or two.)

Gently pat each skeleton leaf dry with a paper towel
or soft cloth. Place each of the damp leaves between
pieces of white paper and flatten in a heavy book
(phone books are good) or in a flower press in
a warm, dry place with good air
circulation. Allow to dry
completely (about two or
three days).

When the skeleton leaves are
pressed and dried completely,
they can be left natural, dyed
or painted, and sealed with a
spray sealer.

Method 2 - The Slow Simmer
(This method includes the bleaching of leaves.)

In a stainless steel pot combine one teaspoon of washing soda and four cups of water. Place several mature leaves in the pot and bring to a full boil. Turn down heat and simmer for 30-60 minutes, or until leaves turn soft and pulpy (it may take more or less time depending on the leaves selected). When the water has cooled, carefully remove the leaves and lay them flat on a newspaper or blotting paper. There are many ways you can remove the pulpy material still clinging to the leaf skeleton. Some people use a dull knife or the edge of a spoon (*gently!*), others rub the leaves with their fingers, still others use a soft brush in an up and down patting motion to dislodge the plant tissue. If you use the soft brush method, do not rub, as you may tear the network of veins (see *Sources*).

Bleaching the Skeletonized Leaves

When the pulpy material has been removed you can bleach the skeletonized leaves by soaking them for 1-2 hours in a solution of two tablespoons of household bleach and one litre of water (work in a well ventilated room). Remove the leaves when the desired lightening is achieved and rinse thoroughly with water. Gently pat each skeleton leaf dry with a paper towel or soft cloth. Place each of the damp leaves between pieces of white paper and flatten in a heavy book (phone books are good) or in a flower press in a warm, dry place with good air circulation. Allow to dry completely (about two or three days).

When the skeleton leaves are pressed and dried completely, they can be left natural, dyed or painted, and sealed with a spray sealer.

*Dyeing and Coloring**

Natural color may be intensified or artificial color introduced to dried plant materials by dyeing or coloring.

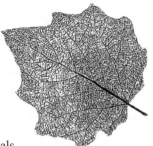

Here are several methods for dyeing or coloring plant materials.

Dip Dyeing

1. <u>Ink or food coloring</u> should be mixed in water to which 1 tablespoon alum per gallon has been added.

2. <u>Fabric dye</u> should be mixed with water to desired strength.

3. <u>Floral dip dyes</u> should be mixed as directed.

   Method: Dip materials in solution until the desired colour is obtained. If the colour becomes too intense accidentally, it is usually possible to lighten it by rinsing it in clear water. Colors will lighten in the drying process. Dry the dyed materials by the preferred method.

Spray Painting

1. <u>Commercial floral sprays:</u> Used as directed, these are not harmful to even the most delicate materials and are available in a wide choice of colors including some metallics. Follow product directions.

2. <u>Ordinary house paints sold in aerosol cans:</u> Use only on heavy textured material such as branches, thick or large leaves, seed pods, and cones. Follow product directions.

Sealing and Finishes

Spray heavy-textured materials with lacquer or varnish to add a shine or a permanent finish. For finer items, canned lacquer may be thinned and brushed on or the materials may be dipped into it. You can choose from a high gloss to a satin finish, depending on your project and your taste.

Your local craft store or hobby shop will also carry a range of sealants and can recommend one for your particular project.

*Portions of this information have been reprinted by permission of the University of Florida, Institute of Food and Agricultural Sciences, Circular 495, Department of Environmental Horticulture, Florida Cooperative Extension Service. Date first printed: November 1981. Revised: June 1997. http://edis.ifas.ufl.edu/EP004

Sources

Two products you can buy that will make all this easier are a microwave flower press, which will dry the skeletonized leaves in minutes rather than days and a soft, multi-bristle fingernail brush. Both are available from *Lee Valley Tools (Canada: 1-800-267-8767, U.S.: 1-800-871-8158, or www.leevalley.com)*. The brushes are approximately 50¢ ($CDN) each and the microwave flower presses are about $20 ($CDN) each.